MW00718997

Praise for
THE BREAKTHROUGH POWER OF
FIRST FRUIT GIVING

"The Breakthrough Power of First Fruit Giving presents a powerful way to exercise our faith. God has done it for me and I fervently believe that He will abundantly bless all who gives Him the first of whatever He bestows upon them in every area of their lives."

Rev. Arthur Jackson, III, Pastor, M.Div.
Antioch Missionary Baptist Church
Miami Gardens, FL

"Pastor Jackson has deconstructed a profound principle that will release the supernatural blessings of God into the lives of all who will put the principles of first fruit giving into practice!"
Dr. C.E. Glover, Pastor
Mount Bethel Baptist Church
Ft. Lauderdale, FL

"God gave His first...His only begotten Son, our Lord and Savior Jesus Christ, as a living sacrifice. In The Breakthrough Power of First Fruit Giving, Pastor Jackson shows us how to integrate into our giving, offerings that honor God with the first of everything He gives to us. Try God with sacrificial gifts of first fruit offerings and watch Him show up and show out in ways that only He can!"
Rev. Donte Hickman, Pastor
Southern Baptist Church
Baltimore, MD

THE BREAKTHROUGH POWER OF
FIRST FRUIT GIVING

Alphonso Jackson, Sr.

Free Flow Publishing
P.O. BOX 924641
Miami, FL 33092
Visit our website at www.freeflow.co

ISBN 978-0-9833463-5-7
Printed in the United States of America

Acknowledgements

God birthed the revelation of *The Breakthrough Power of First Fruit Giving* in my spirit several years ago. Since then, I have devoted many hours studying, researching and teaching this spiritual principle to the body of Christ. It was time well spent and has allowed me to experience God's covenant love in a greater dimension.

This work of ministering about first fruit could only have been made possible through the support and understanding of my family and closest friends. In light of that, I must extend my gratitude and appreciation:

To my precious wife, Dewana Williams Jackson – You have shared me in ministry with so many throughout our entire marriage. I want you to know how much I love you and appreciate your support of me in this endeavor. You are a wonderful wife to me and I'm looking forward to growing old with you. I love you baby.

To my children, Rev. Alphonso, Jr. and Brianna – Thank you for the great sacrifice of sharing your father. I know it has not been easy. Know that I love you both very much.

To my mother, Mary Jackson and my siblings, Minister Gloria Jackson-Davis, Deacon Alex Jackson, Rev. Arthur Jackson, III, Tracy Vickers, and Dr. Cynthia Rains - Thank you for demonstrating love in action by the way we have always stuck together, even during the loss of our greatest hero - our father - the late, but great Rev. Dr. Arthur Jackson, Jr.

To my sister-in-law Kela Williams - Special thanks for your words of encouragement, as you pushed me to pursue the dream of completing this writing. Thanks Monique!

To the greatest church on this side of heaven, the SECOND BAPTIST CHURCH of Richmond Heights in Miami, FL - I don't have the words to describe the incredible love and support you have shown my family and me over the years. You make it so much easier for me to fulfill the Great Commission and carry out the Lord's will for my ministry. Thank you!

Finally, to my many friends and comrades,

local and across this country, who have allowed me to preach, teach and share this powerful revelation of first fruit giving. I pray that whatever the Lord has allowed me to pour into your lives and ministries, will be of a special help and blessing to you as you further the great work of the kingdom. To God be the glory!

And now, most of all, I offer my first book, *The Breakthrough Power of First Fruit Giving* unto the Lord as a first fruit offering in the name of our Lord and Savior Jesus Christ!

FOREWORD

The revelation of God's Word is the single most exhilarating enterprise any man undertakes. As an ardent and passionate student of the Word, Moderator Jackson has demonstrated a uniquely unparalleled accomplishment in *The Breakthrough Power of First Fruit Giving*.

Stewardship is generally the less traveled road of worship. And while the benefits, once realized, joyously overwhelm the believer, the ability to effectively navigate this path can be daunting. Blessed with a great oratorical ability, Pastor Jackson translates this gift into a work deliberately crafted to communicate, illustrate and illuminate this trail to traverse.

Embarking upon this path of first fruit will nourish previously unknown places in your soul. My covenant brother has prepared a feast that will delight the palate of the discerning and will satisfy the soul of the voracious. This will be the text to help transport you to the feet of the Master, to the place of His throne, to the full joy of His respect and His regard. (Genesis 4:4 AMP)

Bishop Victor T. Curry, D. Min.
Founding Senior Pastor
New Birth Baptist Church Cathedral of Faith
International
Miami, FL
Senior Pastor
St. Ruth Missionary Baptist Church
Dania, FL

CONTENTS

Acknowledgements

Foreword by Bishop Victor T. Curry

THE BREAKTHROUGH POWER OF
FIRST FRUIT GIVING

Alphonso Jackson, Sr.

FREE FLOW PUBLISHING

INTRODUCTION

Several years ago, as I undertook my daily meditation, the Lord laid Proverbs 3:9 heavy on my heart. It says:

> *9Honour the LORD with*
> *thy substance, and with*
> *the firstfruits of all thine increase;"*
> *(KJV)*

I had always understood this verse to be in reference to the tithe. As I began to pray, it was revealed to me that first fruit and tithing are not one in the same. I began to research the scripture in great detail. Then, the Lord spoke, telling me that I must pull back the covers of understanding on the awesome teaching of the breakthrough power of first fruit giving.

Once the Lord gave me the revelation, I could not wait to share my first fruit seed with my pastor, Rev. Dr. William H. Copeland of Kankakee, IL. At that time, Pastor Copeland did not have a comprehensive understanding on the subject. However, I asked him to do what the Word of God says in Ezekiel 44:30: to wave my offering before God on my behalf.

That same year, one Sunday afternoon in May, my wife and I were preparing to worship with my brother during his pastoral anniversary. As we were preparing to go, we received a frantic call from one of our members. She exclaimed that our son, Alphonso, Jr., had been in a terrible car accident.

As we drove towards the scene, all I could do was pray, and in so doing, remind God of His promise. Al was our first fruit child. Though we dedicated him back to God after birth, when I received the first fruit revelation, we rededicated him to God as a first fruit offering. I just kept pleading the blood of Jesus over my son, asking the favor of God to be upon him.

As we reached the scene of the accident, we could see from a distance that his car was flipped on its side in the middle of the road. Fear immediately gripped my heart. The idea of my son being trapped inside the car nearly overwhelmed me. I continued to resist the urge to panic and prayed, "Lord, spare my son."

When I got to the barricade, my son saw me, scrambled from the car and ran towards me! He wasn't injured at all! We embraced, cried and thanked God for His favor and mercy. The car was totaled, but neither my son, nor my God-son (Robert Cordy) who was a passenger in the car, had any noticeable scratches. Futhermore, even Al, Jr's glasses were intact: neither cracked nor scratched! We later learned that the car had flipped over three times before finally resting on its side!

Some people saw the car and said the boys were extremely lucky. But, we, as people of faith know that luck had absolutely nothing to do with it. What a mighty God we serve! I praise Jehovah for the breakthrough power of first fruit giving!

Since receiving my revelation from the Lord, I have studied the principle of First Fruit giving extensively. I have read what others have said on the subject, including Rev. Dr. Creflo Dollar, Paula White and many others.

I have accepted the charge from the Lord to shine this light upon His people, realizing that it would not be readily recieved by everyone. However, sensing that the mantel of first fruit teaching had fallen upon me, it compelled me to pray and prepare.

I have already personally seen and experienced

the many blessings of first fruit giving, and I believe wholeheartedly, that even in a failing economy, this teaching will be a great blessing to all who honor God by sowing first fruit seed.

As believers, we must understand that giving is a kingdom principle which goes beyond the tithe. As children of the most high God, He who blesses us with all things, we must be willing and cheerful givers. Giving is a divine discipline of the Kingdom of God.

The Biblical Principle of First Fruit exists for the purpose of enriching every area of our lives. As we venture into this new territory filled with promise and possibility, there are several key scriptures related to this principle that should serve as a light to illuminate your path towards first fruit giving:

> *38Give and it will be given to you. A good measure, pressed down, shaken together and running over, will be poured into your lap. For with the measure you use, it will be measured to you.*
>
> *Luke 6:38 (KJV)*

> *12For if there be first a willing mind, it is accepted according to that a man hath, and not according to that he hath not.*
>
> *II Corinthians 8:12 (KJV)*

> *17And thou say in thine heart, My power and the might of mine hand hath gotten me this wealth. 18But thou shalt remember the LORD thy God: for it is he that giveth thee power to get wealth, that he may establish his covenant which*

*he sware unto thy fathers, as it is
this day.*

> *Deuteronomy 8:17-18 (KJV)*

God's word is true! The principle of giving requires that as you give, your storehouse will not only be refilled, but will overflow overwhelmingly, thus enabling you to continue to give.

Practicing the Principle of First Fruit will enable you to experience the breakthrough power of God!

Rev. Dr. Alphonso Jackson, Sr., Pastor
Second Baptist Church
Miami, FL

CHAPTER 1
THE FIRST FRUIT PRINCIPLE

The term "first" itself is defined as being before all others in place, order and rank; the beginning, chief or principle thing. First Fruit is a biblical principle ordained by God. It literally means *"a promise to come."* The principle proclaims that the first of everything belongs to God. And everything means everything. The first moments of everyday are first fruit moments. The first day of every week is the first fruit Sunday. The first month of every New Year, is the first fruit month. The

first hour of your day is the first fruit hour. The first child

out of the womb is the first fruit child. The Bible speaks

of this principle very clearly:

> *11After the LORD brings you into the land of the Canaanites and gives it to you, as he promised on oath to you and your forefathers, 12 you are to give over to the LORD the first offspring of every womb. All the firstborn males of your livestock belong to the LORD. 13Redeem with a lamb every firstborn donkey, but if you do not redeem it, break its neck. Redeem every firstborn among your sons.*
>
> *Exodus 13:11-13 (NIV)*

Every area in your life where increase manifests,

that increase belongs to God. The first establishes the blessing on the rest. What you do with the first, sets precedence for the remainder.

Whenever and wherever increase occurs for the first time in your life, first fruit giving offers that increase to God. When God accepts the First Fruit offering, He sanctifies the whole.

> *16Now if the first handful of dough offered as the First Fruit is consecrated (holy), so is the whole mass and if the root is consecrated (holy), so are the branches.*
>
> *Romans 11:16 (AV)*

The first of the very first is the best of all firstfruit, and the best of every sacrifice of every kind.

Whenever an increase shows up in your life, it belongs to God. In Numbers 18:12, it says:

> *[12]I give you all the finest olive oil and all the finest new wine and grain they give the LORD as the First Fruit of their harvest. (NIV)*

The Lord specifically instructed Moses to present his first ground meal to Him as an offering from the threshing floor when he entered the promised land and partook of the fruit of the land. Speaking directly to Moses, in Numbers 15:21, God further directed him as such, saying:

> *[21]Throughout the generations to come you are to give this offering to the LORD from the first of your ground meal.*

Numbers 15:21 (NIV)

In essence, the first part of the meal was to be offered up to God as a symbol that it all belonged to Him. Of the bread presented to the Lord, the cornmeal for the bread was taken from the ground meal. However, that bread was formed, baked and then presented as a first fruit offering. Since it was set apart to the Lord first, the whole harvest was, therefore, sanctified.

So it is in nature as well. With a tree, the root comes first and its branches sprout later. The nature of that tree specimen is attributed to its roots. When a gardener went into the field or vineyard when the fruit was ripening, he was to mark that which he observed as the most ripe and set it aside to sacrifice for first fruit.

Whether it was wheat, barley, grapes, figs, pomegranates, olives, or dates, for example, the farmer would put them in a basket and present them to God in the place where His name was worshipped. This was done not out of fear of an angry God, rather, out of a spirit of gratitude and thanksgiving for all the Lord had done.

The initial harvest belongs to God.

In God's Holy word, the principle of First Fruit was not limited to vegetation. First fruit is found throughout the Bible, and deals with the firsts of all things. God claims the right to every first including, but certainly not limited to the first of the crops, every first-born male of herds and flocks, and every first-born male child. This tells us that every first is to be devoted

to God through His covenant. This was demonstrated

routinely in Biblical times.

I Kings 17 tells of a widow woman who was

gathering sticks to build a fire to cook what she thought

would be her last meal. The prophet Elijah, showed up

and instructed her on God's order which is to put Him

first.

When Elijah arrived in Zarephath, he arrived

at the right time, meeting the right woman, who lived

outside the land of Israel. The Gospel of Luke records

that although there were many widows in Israel at the

time, Elijah was sent specifically to her.

25I assure you that there were

> *many widows in Israel in Elijah's*
> *time, when the sky was shut for three*
> *and a half years and there was a*
> *severe famine throughout the land.*
> *26Yet Elijah was not sent to any of*
> *them, but to a widow in Zarephath in*
> *the region of Sidon.*
>
> *Luke 4:25-26 (NIV)*

This meeting at the gate was providential, and by no means coincidental.

Elijah requested a drink of water and the widow asked no questions. She prepared a vessel for him. Then, in verse 11b, he called to her to bring him a morsel of bread.

She responded with her reality, saying, she didn't have enough to share and resources were minimal.

To emphasize the severity of her situation, she added,

"I'm gathering sticks for my last meal."

Elijah told her:

> *13Don't worry about a thing. Go ahead and do what you've said. But first make a small biscuit for me and bring it back here. Then go ahead and make a meal from what's left for you and your son. 14This is the word of the God of Israel: 'The jar of flour will not run out and the bottle of oil will not become empty before God sends rain on the land and ends this drought.*

> *1 Kings 17:13-14 (MSG)*

The Bible says, upon hearing those words, she

took the man of God at his word, put God first, and did

what he asked of her. The breakthough power of God then manifested in her life! The Bible says that every time the widow dipped into the barrel, there was meal in it. Every time she scooped into the barrel, there was always a supply!

The widow started the day gathering sticks for what she was sure to be her last supper. But God! By day's end, she was miraculously eating from a barrel that perpetually provided her nutritional needs. Why? Because she put God first, as the prophet Elijah instructed her to do. What a mighty God we serve!

For us today, anytime a first occurs in our lives, it represents harvest and therefore, belongs to God. Consider it your first fruit and understand that offering it to God will bless the rest of all that is to come.

> *23Whatever you do, work at it*
> *with all your heart, as working for*
> *the Lord, not for human masters,*
>
> *Colossians 3:23 (NIV)*

CHAPTER 2
FIRST THINGS FIRST

In the Hebrew, first fruit is translated as bikkurim - a promise to come. You may be surprised to learn this, but the *Feast of First Fruits* is mentioned in the Bible second only to the Passover. To reemphasize: the Passover is the only Jewish celebration mentioned throughout the Word of God more than the *Feast of First Fruits.*

In Biblical times, each family among the

Israelites was required to harvest the first fruit of the crops and bring them into the temple. The first fruit was then presented to the High Priest in thanksgiving, according to the God of Israel. Furthermore, this act of gratitude was done in recognition of God's continued provision and blessing for their sacrifice. Once the offering of the first fruit had been made, the rest of the harvest was considered to be sanctified and the people could enjoy it freely.

First fruit giving empowers us to access and manage the wealth of resources God has already provided. To embark on this journey, a self-assessment is in order. You must have a heart-to-heart with yourself about where you are in your life. You must truthfully determine the "land" in which you live psychologically:

> Do you exist in **Egypt**: the land of never
> enough.

> Do you wander in the **Wilderness**: the land of
> just enough.

> Or, are you a conquest in **Canaan**: the land of
> more than enough.

Egypt, the Wilderness, and Canaan each represent a distinct point of view which will dictate your life's results.

EGYPT
THE LAND OF NEVER ENOUGH

Those who choose to live in "Egypt - The Land of Never Enough," never seem to have a sufficient amount or quantity of anything. They simply never have enough. Something is always lacking. Something is always due or past due. They are always a day late and a dollar short. Furthermore, they always seem to have their hand out, ready to receive, but hardly ever do they give.

Those who choose to live in "Egypt" refuse to trust God with the tithe, or any other sacrificial offering. And true to form, they will be the ones who are skeptical of first fruit giving, regardless of what the Bible says.

No matter how many resources are directed their way, it is never enough for the inhabitants of "Egypt." Furthermore, they tend to breed dysfunctional families and find themselves in fragmented friendships.

They are always in crisis-mode and stress constantly weighs them down.

Let it be known: the real problem with the habitants of "The Land of Never Enough" is not finances, family, friends, nor fatigue. The heart of the problem is a lack of faith. The root of their issue is their refusal to surrender and trust God with and in all things. Not trusting God with the resources He has blessed you with will keep you bound and suppressed in "The Land of Never Enough."

THE WILDERNESS
THE LAND OF JUST ENOUGH

Those who live in "The Land of Just Enough" will give, but do so grudgingly. They tip, but do not actually tithe. They experience moments of happiness, but no sincere joy.

People in the "Wilderness" know there's infinite potential to soar in life, but they are not committed to doing what it takes to ascend to the next level and beyond. They tend to live from paycheck to paycheck, settling for just enough resources to stay afloat.

Those who live in "The Land of Just Enough" routinely make vows of poverty unknowingly, saying things like "I don't want to be rich, I just want to have enough to do this...I just want to have enough to do that." As a result, guess what? They have exactly what they say they want and nothing more.

With the wilderness wanderers, their frequent

frustration is a persistent reminder that just enough is really never enough.

CANAAN
THE LAND OF MORE THAN ENOUGH

The "Canaan Conquerors" live in "The Land of More Than Enough." They are determined to take God at His word. They walk by faith and not by sight.

They have a firm understanding that the seed can never and will never be greater than the harvest. Even beyond that, the "Canaan Conquerers" recognize and believe in the power the seed possesses. They understand that when they sow good seed into fertile ground, they will receive a bountiful harvest.

Those in "The Land of More Than Enough"

believe what God says, even when they can't see what God says. They have tremendous faith. They speak what God says, until they start seeing what God says.

Where do you dwell today and where do you want to be:

Are you existing in Egypt?

Are you wandering in the Wilderness?

Are you conquering Canaan?

I choose Canaan! Won't you? Let's look at the children of Israel as an example.

When the children of Israel were wandering in the wilderness for forty years, God miraculously fed them with manna from heaven until they reached the border of Canaan. (Exodus 16:35) It was God's grace that allowed the manna to rain for four decades. It was because of God's mercy that the manna nourished and sustained the Israelites in the wilderness for generations.

The Lord could have caused it to cease long before, especially after they provoked Him through their lack of appreciation for God's provision. They complained bitterly. They despised the manna. They even diminished the miracle of the manna, calling it light bread!

The children of Israel blatantly spoke against God. To add insult to injury, they challenged Moses, their God-sent leader, saying in Numbers 21:5, *Why have you brought us up out of Egypt to die in the desert? There is no bread! There is no water! And we detest this miserable food! (NIV)*

God knows all and sees all. He knew their frustration. He knew that their limited vision disabled them from seeing the blessings He had in store for them, but, God looked beyond their faults and saw their needs. He made provision for them by allowing manna to rain from the heavens.

> [11]*And on that same day they ate the produce of the land: unleavened cakes and parched grain.* [12]*And the manna ceased on the day after they ate of the produce of the land; and the Israelites had manna no more, but they ate of the fruit of the land of Canaan that year.*
>
> *John 5:11-12 (ESV)*

After 40 years of divine provision, the manna suddenly stopped. However, God did not discontinue supplying their daily needs. He was preparing to feed the children of Israel another way.

After eating of the produce of Canaan, I can see the Israelites rising early the next morning to gather the manna. But to their surprise, the manna had ceased. The miracle of the manna ceased when God knew the Israelites could manage the task of gathering food for themselves. You don't need manna when you can manage.

The take-away from this story for us today is, when the manna ceases to rain in our lives, we must trust and believe that it is not a sign that we have been abandoned by God. We are His children and the Bible is crystal clear in telling us that He will never leave us, nor forsake us.

When the manna appears to stop flowing in your life, it is a signal that God is preparing to saturate you with blessings that you will not have room enough to receive. Rest assured that the power of first fruit giving will open the windows of heaven and pour out blessings that will absolutely overwhelm you with amazement, joy and gratitude.

Chapter 3
The Purpose of First Fruit

Planting first fruit seed is a reflection of our faith. It is faith in action, believing that God will provide in our time of need, be they great or small. Your sacrifice speaks volumes in demonstrating to God that you believe in His promise of harvest, and you, therefore, are sowing seeds to prompt the harvest in due time.

It is important that you are clear that God is not trying to extract anything from you through your first fruit sacrifice. Rather, it is a method for Him to bless you. The two-fold purpose of first fruit is to release praises unto God and to release blessings from God unto us.

In Deuteronomy 26:1-11, we glimpse a beautiful ceremony in which the Israelites brought to God a portion of the first ripened fruit as an offering.

> *[1]When you have come into the land which the Lord your God gives you as an inheritance and possess it and live in it, [2]You shall take some of the first of all the produce of the soil which you harvest from the land the Lord your God gives you and put it in a basket, and go to the place [the sanctuary] which the Lord your God has chosen as the abiding place for*

His Name [and His Presence]. ³And you shall go to the priest who is in office in those days, and say to him, I give thanks this day to the Lord your God that I have come to the land which the Lord swore to our fathers to give us. ⁴And the priest shall take the basket from your hand and set it down before the altar of the Lord your God. ⁵And you shall say before the Lord your God, A wandering and lost Aramean ready to perish was my father [Jacob], and he went down into Egypt and sojourned there, few in number, and he became there a nation, great, mighty, and numerous. ⁶And the Egyptians treated us very badly and afflicted us and laid upon us hard bondage. ⁷And when we cried to the Lord, the God of our fathers, the Lord heard our voice

FIRST FISH

There was a knock on the door of the hut occupied by a missionary in Africa. Answering, there stood one of the native boys holding a very big fish. The boy said, "Reverend, you taught us what first fruit is, so here, I've brought you my first fruit."

As the missionary gratefully took the fish, he questioned the young lad. "If this is your first fruit, where are the other fish?" At this, the boy beamed and said, "Oh, they're still back in the river. I'm going back to catch them now!"

and looked on our affliction and our labor and our [cruel] oppression; [8]And the Lord brought us forth out of Egypt with a mighty hand and with an outstretched arm, and with great (awesome) power and with signs and with wonders; [9]And He brought us into this place and gave us this land, a land flowing with milk and honey. [10]And now, behold, I bring the first fruit of the ground which You, O Lord, have given me. And you shall set it down before the Lord your God and worship before the Lord your God; [11]And you and the Levite and the stranger and the sojourner among you shall rejoice in all the good which the Lord your God has given you and your household.

Deuteronomy 26:1-11 (AMP)

The Israelites' first fruit offering was acknowledgment that all the produce of the land came from God and was an expression of gratitude for His goodness. As Moses presented his offering to the Lord, he was to review God's gracious dealings with His people by delivering them from oppression in Egypt and ushering them into the bountiful land He promised them.

This was intended to continually remind the people of the kindness of God, in preserving them through so many difficulties and literally fulfilling the promises He had made to them. Because God was the provider of all their blessings, the first fruit of the land was consecrated to Him, the author of every good and perfect gift.

When we sow the first fruit seed, we release praises to God. Some mistakenly think that we sow the first fruit seed to get more from the Lord, but there is a song that says, "If He never does anything else, He's already done enough!" Sowing the first fruit seed is an act of praise and gratitude to God.

RELEASE GOD'S BLESSINGS

One of many ways to define the word honor is: to make heavy, to weigh down and carry weight, to prefer, to give preference to, to respect, to give a level of importance, to highly esteem. You honor God when you allow His Word to carry so much weight in your life that nothing and no one can sway you from the Word.

We must honor God, not just with our bodies and spirits, which are His, but with our resources as well, which also belong to Him.

> *⁹Honor the Lord with your possessions, and with the First Fruit of all your increase; ¹⁰So your barns will be filled with plenty, And your vats (freshly squeezed grape juice) will overflow with new wine.*
>
> *Proverbs 3:9-10 (AV)*

Whatever God sends us in the way of prosperity, the first portion of it should always be presented back to Him. Remember, when the first portion is sacrificed, the remainder is sanctified. According to Exodus 13:11-13, when it is withheld, God's curse is upon the whole.

When the possessor of heaven and earth brought you into being and placed you in this world, He placed you here not as the owner, but as a steward. He entrusted you, for a season, with goods of all kinds. However, the sole ownership still rests in Him and can never be alienated from Him. You are not your own, but His. Likewise, all that you possess and enjoy belong to Him as well.

CAIN AND ABEL

The story of Cain and Abel illustrates giving from the heart versus giving from the hand. The act of giving in and of itself is insufficient to be called sacrificial. Understand that it is possible to give and still not honor God. Even as early as the Book of Genesis, the Bible gives us a clear example of gracious first fruit giving and begrudged first fruit giving.

Genesis 4:4-5 tells the story of Cain and Abel, the first two sons of Adam and Eve, and their efforts to worship God. Abel gave the Lord a first fruit offering consisting of portions of fat from the firstborn of his flock.

His offering wasn't aesthetically beautiful. In fact, it was bloody. But, the Lord looked with favor on Abel and his offering. The Word says, "The Lord had respect unto Abel and to his offering." In other words, God saw Abel's heart and accepted what was in his hands. Abel's attitude was this: everything I have belongs to God and there is nothing I have that God can not get!

Abel placed God first, in the right place. He made a first fruit offering and in that act of worship, his faith demonstrated and acknowledged that it was not by his own hand that he was a prosperous shepherd, but, by the hand of God, he was blessed. Abel was counted a righteous man.

Conversely, let's examine Abel's brother, Cain. He is a great example of someone who gives an offering that doesn't honor God. You may know someone like Cain - someone who gives God what they want to give, instead of what He requires. As a result of Cain's approach to giving, he experienced drastically different results.

> *⁵But on Cain and his offering he did*
> *not look with favor. So Cain was very*
> *angry, and his face was downcast.*
> *Genesis 4:5 (NIV)*

Many make the argument that Cain's offering was rejected because of the lack of blood. Understandably so, because, the Word of God speaks of the essential role that blood plays in our salvation.

> *²²In fact, the law requires that nearly*
> *everything be cleansed with blood,*
> *and without the shedding of blood*
> *there is no forgiveness."*
> *Hebrews 9:22 (NIV)*

And, yes, we know that Abel's offering did involve bloodshed. But, we can not overlook, nor dismiss the fact that Cain's offering was from cursed ground.

A first fruit offering is not a sin offering. However, coming before God as he did, it was as if Cain was presenting his offering based on his own worthiness, rather than by God's mercy. He presented the work of his own toil, of his own hands, no doubt bringing choice fruit for his offering. It was perhaps presented beautifully. That may all be true. However, understand that God is more concerned about what's in our hearts as opposed to what's is in our hands.

In fact, it really wasn't about what Cain gave. What mattered was why he gave. Cain's offering reflected and revealed the condition of a "heart defect."

If your heart isn't right, no matter what gift you present to God, it will not honor Him. Abel's offering no doubt was consumed by fire while Cain's offering lay coldly upon the altar.

God does not care what's in your hand if it doesn't line up with what's in your heart. When God honors you, he will surely honor your gifts.

Abel's gift reminds us that first fruit requires faith. Abel demonstrated just that. As the writer of Hebrews recorded, by faith Abel offered God a better sacrifice than Cain. By faith, Abel was deemed a righteous man.

The writer further expounded on how essential faith is:

> *6And without faith it is impossible to please God, because anyone who comes to him must believe that he exists and that he rewards those who earnestly seek him.*
>
> *Hebrews 11:6 (NIV)*

The first fruit offering is faith-based. We must have faith in the fact that the root governs the rest. We must have faith that giving God the whole of the first releases blessings on the rest. Finally, we must trust and believe that God will reward of those who earnestly seek Him.

CHAPTER 4
THE ANNUAL FIRST FRUIT SEED

As children of God, we, too are instructed to set aside the first fruit offering at the beginning of each year and bring it before the Lord. Nehemiah 10:35-36 says:

> *35We also assume responsibility for bringing to the house of the LORD each year the firstfruits of our crops and of every fruit tree. 36As it is also written in the Law, we will bring the firstborn of our sons and of our cattle, of our herds and of our flocks*

to the house of our God, to the priests
ministering there.

Nehemiah 10:35-36 (NIV)

Now, I know you're probably not a gardener
in the Biblical sense of the word. You probably don't
own a herd, nor a flock. So how can first fruit giving be
applied in our lives today, that we, too, may be blessed
and bless others?

It can be the first hours of your day, the first
of your family, your time and your talents. The first
establishes the blessing on the rest.

The first fruit offering is also the first of any
kind of revenue stream or increase. For instance, if
you receive a pay raise, the first time you receive a pay

check including the raise, your first fruit offering would be the difference between the previous pay and the new pay. After you give your first fruit, then you tithe on the rest.

Remember we must, *"seek first the Kingdom of God and His righteousness and all these things shall be added to you." Matthew 6:33 (NIV)*

The first belongs to God and it goes beyond money. January of every year is set aside as the first fruit month. Each year, my church, Second Baptist Church in Miami, FL, embarks on a *Trinity Fast*, setting aside the month of January as a time of private and corporate fasting, praying and giving. The *Trinity Fast* asks each member to sacrifice three things that he or she enjoys eating or doing for the entire month. In addition, we commit to reading one chapter per day from the book of Proverbs - 31 chapters in 31 days. We also pray over the scriptures from those chapters. Finally, of course, we give to God our sacrificial seed of the first revenue stream of the year.

Well, by now, you already understand that January is the first month of the year, which establishes what will happen in the duration of the entire year. Our sacrifice speaks of our faith in a promise of things to come. The more seed that I can get out of my hand and into God's hands, the sooner and greater will be my Harvest!

By applying the first fruit principle at the

beginning of each year, you acknowledge the fact that the Lord has been merciful and kind in the previous year, and you are acting upon your fervent belief that his unmerited favor will be extended to you throughout the year ahead.

God says first things belong to Him in order to establish redeeming covenant with everything that comes after. In God's pattern, whatever is first, establishes the rest. Again, the first is the root from which the rest is determined.

Let me explain practically what first fruit financial giving looks like in two scenarios.

If you had no revenue and the Lord blessed you with an income, the very first time the increase appears in your life, it belongs to God.

In the second example, if you had an established revenue of $500 per week and you received a pay increase of an additional $50 per week, the very first $50 increase you receive would be offered to God as a first fruit offering. Therefore, with that week's earnings, you would pay your tithes on the $500, and donate the additional $50 increase to God. As follows, with the next week's salary, your tithes would be paid on the entire $550.

The Bible is so clear in its intent for first fruit to be sacrificed. Exodus 13:13 says it is better to destroy your first fruit than to use any of it for your own personal gain. God considers first things to be holy and devoted to Him. All holy things belong to God. Touching holy things will often bring judgment to the offender.

Let us look to the city of Jericho to illustrate this point. The city of Jericho was the first city that Israel entered into and conquered. Since God lays claim to all firsts, He ordered Israel to kill it, burn it, or put it into the Lord's treasure.

> [18]*But keep away from the devoted things, so that you will not bring about your own destruction by taking any of them. Otherwise you will make the camp of Israel liable to destruction and bring trouble on it.* [19]*All the silver and gold and the articles of bronze and iron are sacred to the LORD and must go into his treasury.*

Joshua 6:18-19 (NIV)

When Israel defeated other cities, they were able to keep the spoils of victory. The book of Joshua chapter 8, verse 2 says, *"You shall do to Ai and its king as you did to Jericho and its king, except that you may carry off their plunder and livestock for yourselves."* *(NIV)*

This was not the case with Jericho because God always lays claim to the first.

In Joshua chapter 7, verses 20-21, it tells us that Achan, an Israelite, heard his commander give the order that all the spoils in Jericho were to be devoted to the Lord and were to go into His treasury. Since Jericho was Israel's first victory in Canaan, the first fruit of the wealth belonged to the Lord. But, Achan disobeyed.

The Bible says Achan saw, he coveted, and he took. His disobedience was sinful and led to his death.

Achan's first mistake was to look at the "spoils" a second time. He probably couldn't help seeing them the first time, but he should have never looked again and considered taking them. The second mistake Achan made was to reclassify the treasures, calling them "spoils." That, they were not! In fact, they were part of the Lord's treasury and wholly dedicated to Him. They didn't belong to Achan, nor even to Israel. They belonged to God.

When God identifies something in a special way, we have no right to change it. In our world today, including the religious world, people are rewriting God's dictionary. The Bible says *"Woe unto them that call evil good, and good evil; that put darkness for light, and light for darkness; that put bitter for sweet, and sweet for bitter!" Isaiah 5:20 (KJV)*

When confronted in Joshua chapter 7, Achan replied:

> *[20]It is true! I have sinned against the LORD, the God of Israel. This is what I have done: [21]When I saw in the plunder a beautiful robe from Babylonia, two hundred shekels of silver and a wedge of gold weighing fifty shekels, I coveted them and took them. They are hidden in the ground inside my tent, with the silver underneath.*

Joshua 7:20-21 (NIV)

Achan paid a heavy price for coveting the things of the world. He brought defeat to Israel and death to himself and his family.

If we keep God's Word before our eyes, we won't begin to look in the wrong direction and do the wrong things. The lesson found within Achan's story is, he took what belonged to the Lord and hid it among his own. Many of us today are still guilty of pilfering from the Lord, and hiding it for our own selfish interests. Be careful about how you handle holy things!

CHAPTER 5
APPOINTED AND ANNOINTED TO BLESS

At this point, you may be wondering what happens once the first fruit offering is given unto the Lord. Well, the God we serve is a God of order. As such, in His house, he has designated the Shepherds of His house to be the vessel through which first fruit gifts are presented.

The Word of God, in Ezekiel, shows that first fruit offerings must go through the priests.

30The best of all the First Fruit and

> *of all your special gifts will belong*
> *to the priests. You are to give them*
> *the first portion of your ground meal*
> *so that a blessing may rest on your*
> *household.*
>
> *Ezekiel 44:30 (NIV)*

In God's plan for first fruit giving, He appointed the priest to be actively involved in the blessing of His people. The people are to bring their first fruit to the priest, who waves it before the Lord on their behalf in faith that the blessings may remain in their house. *(Ezekiel 44:30)*

In the book of the second law, Deuteronomy, Chapter 26:1-4 Moses spent much time articulating clear details as he repeated the laws God had given

Israel.

Once the first fruit offering was given to the priest, they were to proclaim the story of Abraham's journey into Egypt, and how his descendants became a great nation which resulted in their enslavement. Also, as told in Deuteronomy 26:8-10, they would testify about the mighty hand of the Lord that delivered them from Egypt.

The pastor's role in the lives of God's people is vital. Leviticus 6:12-13, records that it was the priest's responsibility to keep the fire continually burning upon the altar. Because of this sacrifice, the people knew that they did not have to wait for a certain day or hour to offer their sacrifice when a trespass had been committed. The altar was always open and the fire was always burning. Today, pastors keep the fire burning in the house of worship and in the hearts of mankind.

The principle of first fruit giving can not be activated independent of the priest. God has chosen to actively involve the priest in the release of blessings for His people. The people are to bring the first fruit of their increase to the man of God, that he may wave it before God on their behalf. (Leviticus 23:9-10) This process causes the blessings to rest or remain in their house, as stated in Ezekiel 44:30.

Therefore, first fruit giving is exercised by the congregants presenting the offering to the priest, who has the latitude to use the offering based on how the Lord leads him or her, for the upbuilding of the kingdom.

Today's equivalent to the priest is the man of God with whom you are in covenant - your pastor. In the Old Testament, the offerings were given to the priest and Levites so they could be devoted to the work of the Lord, carrying out His instructions for the people.

The Bible says that God blessed the Levite priests with first fruit offerings.

When Joshua distributed the allotments in the Promise Land, the tribe of Levites received none. The Lord was to be their portion.

It is important to note that all priests were Levites, but not all Levites were priests. Yet, God did not leave the priests' well-being up to the benevolence of the people. He put guidelines in place for the other tribes to support the work that the priests and Levites performed spiritually on their behalf daily.

In Deuteronomy 18:1-5, Moses issued the guidelines for the priests and Levites concerning the first fruit. Moses gave the Law of God to the people of God.

> [1]*The priests, who are Levites-- indeed the whole tribe of Levi--are to have no allotment or inheritance with Israel. They shall live on the offerings made to the LORD by fire, for that is their inheritance. [2]They shall have no inheritance among their brothers; the LORD is their inheritance, as he promised them.*

> *³This is the share due the priests from the people who sacrifice a bull or a sheep: the shoulder, the jowls and the inner parts. ⁴You are to give them the First Fruit of your grain, new wine and oil, and the first wool from the shearing of your sheep, ⁵for the LORD your God has chosen them and their descendants out of all your tribes to stand and minister in the LORD's name always.*
>
> *Deuteronomy 18:1-5 (NIV)*

What was the significance of this Old Testament method of giving the first fruit offering to the man of God? How exactly did that benefit the one who brought the offering?

Giving to the man of God is the key, as found in

the Word, in the book of Ezekiel:

> [30]*And the first of all the firstfruits of all kinds, and every offering of all kinds from all your offerings, shall belong to the priests. You shall also give to the priest the first of your coarse meal and bread dough, that a blessing may rest on your house.*
>
> *Ezekiel 44:30 (AMP)*

Notice that this is not a one-time blessing. Nor are the blessings limited and short-term. The scripture says the blessing will "rest" in your house. The testimonies of those who have experienced the blessings of first fruit giving continue far beyond the time of the offering. This is a direct result of the priest's - or man of God's - connection to your breakthrough blessing!

When the man of God receives your first fruit offering and waves it before the Lord, it is a means of presenting it to God. His prayer over the offering releases the blessings of the Lord and covers the house of the one who presented the offering.

The Bible says, the blessings will rest upon your house. In reading this, we tend to think of the physical building in which we live and dwell. However, the Hebrew term for house or household is interpreted as family, lineage, children, grandchildren, and generation after generation.

And so it is, that once the first fruit offering is given to the priest, the blessings of God are activated in the life of the giver. The priest then has the discretion of using the first fruit in the manner the Lord has led him to use it. Like the tithe, it is Holy unto the Lord.

First fruit giving is about the giver and what God will or already has done as a result of their faithfulness. As with the tithe, when the first fruit is given with the right spirit, and the right attitude, the blessings of God will flow exceedingly, abundantly, more than you could ever ask or think.

The Pastor must also be charged to regard the first fruit as Holy onto God, using the sacrifice to further Kingdom ministries. The scripture is transparent in its explanation of why first fruits are placed in the hands of the man of God.

- Give to the man of God because of his anointing:

> *8And the LORD spoke unto Aaron, Behold, I also have given thee the charge of mine heave offerings of all the hallowed things of the children of Israel; unto thee have I given them by reason of the anointing, and to thy sons, by an ordinance for ever.*
>
> *Numbers 18:8 (KJV)*

- Give to the man of God because he's chosen:

> *5for the LORD your God has chosen them and their descendants out of all your tribes to stand and minister in the LORD's name always.*
>
> *Deuteronomy 18:5 (NIV)*

In Acts 20:28, the Bible says that God has anointed and chosen the pastor by the Holy Spirit, to be the overseers over the flock of God.

I must acknowledge that some people are skeptical about sowing the first fruit seed to the priest. For them, they may not mind sowing the seed, but not to the priest. However, the priest is your God connection. We must trust the God in the priest to further the Kingdom through the first fruit seed.

CHAPTER 6
FIRST FRUIT-
A TIMELESS SACRIFICE

Some have attempted to limit the First Fruit

Principle to Old Testament teaching. In essence, this

would negate its relevance and application to modern

times. However, the Word of God shows us that first

fruit can not be limited to the Old Testament. There are

many scriptures in the New Testament that affirm the

doctrine of first fruit:

> [16]*If the part of the dough offered as*
> *First Fruit is holy, then the whole batch*
> *is holy; if the root is holy, so are the*

branches.

Romans 11:16 (NIV)

⁵And salute the church that is in their house. Salute Epaenetus my beloved, who is the first-fruit of Asia unto Christ.

Romans 16:5 (NKJV)

²⁰But now hath Christ been raised from the dead, the First Fruit of them that are asleep. ²¹For since by man came death, by man came also the resurrection of the dead. ²²For as in Adam all die, so also in Christ shall all be made alive. ²³But each in his own order: Christ the First Fruit; then they that are Christ's, at his coming.

I Corinthians 15:20-23 (KJV)

¹⁵Now I beseech you, brethren (ye

know the house of Stephanas, that it is the First Fruit of Achaia, and that they have set themselves to minister unto the saints),

I Corinthians 16:15 (KJV)

[18]Of his own will he brought us forth by the word of truth, that we should be a kind of First Fruit of his creatures.

James 1:18 (NKJV)

[4]These are those who did not defile themselves with women, for they kept themselves pure. They follow the Lamb wherever he goes. They were purchased from among men and offered as First Fruit to God and the Lamb.

Revelation 14:4 (NIV)

As evidenced above, the New Testament has much to say about first fruit giving. The Apostle Paul wrote perhaps the most compelling text on the matter. In I Corinthians 15:20 he recognizes Jesus himself as a first fruit offering.

> [20] *But Christ has indeed been raised from the dead, the first fruit of those who have fallen asleep.* [21] *For since death came through a man, the resurrection of the dead comes also through a man.* [22] *For as in Adam all die, so in Christ all will be made alive.* [23] *But each in his own turn: Christ, the firstfruit; then, when he comes, those who belong to him.*
>
> *I Corinthians 15:20-23 (NIV)*

The New Testament fulfilled what the Old Testament revealed.

As a matter of fact, the birth of Jesus was a fulfillment of the first fruit principle.

Since God gave the firstborn, who then bore the curse, so the rest of the harvest could be blessed? Yes, our Lord and Savior, Jesus Christ. John 3:16-17 says *"For God so loved the world that he gave his one and only Son, that whoever believes in him shall not perish but have eternal life. [17]For God did not send his Son into the world to condemn the world, but to save the world through him." (NIV)*

Furthermore, Jesus died on Passover as the Lamb of God - the sheaf of first fruit. He arose from

FOOD FOR THOUGHT

There are ten bananas in the bunch. One banana is symbolically given to God and nine bananas remain. This is an illustration of tithing. Giving ten percent of your bunch is acknowledging the fact that it all belongs to Him and that we manage the resources that are available to us.

First Fruit is giving God the entire bunch the first time you receive the bananas and believing God when He said the first shall set the precedence for the remainder. It's believing that God is able to do exceedingly, abundantly, above all that you ask or think according to power that works within you.

the dead, three days later, on the first day of the week!
When the priest waved the sheaf of the first fruit before
the Lord, it was a sign that the entire harvest belonged
to Him.

When Jesus was raised from the dead, it was
God's assurance to us that we shall also be raised one
day as part of that future harvest. The first fruit has
the power to dictate what the rest of the harvest will
become. What we start with is what the rest will be.

FIRST FRUIT VS. THE TITHE

First fruit may sound similar to tithing. Some
think they are one in the same. However, there are
definite distinctions between the two.

First fruit is introduced for the first time in

Genesis 4, with Abel's offering to the Lord.

> *4And Abel, he also brought of the*
> *firstlings of his flock and of the fat*
> *thereof. And the LORD had respect*
> *unto Abel and to his offering...*
> *Genesis 4:4 KJV*

Tithing first appears in the scripture in Genesis

14, with Abraham and Melchizedek.

> *18And Melchizedek King of Salem*
> *brought forth bread and wine: and*
> *he was the priest of the most high*
> *God. 19And he blessed him, and said,*
> *Blessed be Abram of the most high*
> *God, possessor of heaven and earth:*
> *20And blessed be the most high God,*
> *which hath delivered thine enemies*
> *into thy hand. And he gave him tithes*

of all.

Genesis 14:18-20 (KJV)

First fruit represents the first of the first, while tithing represents ten percent of all income. Practically speaking, tithing offers a total of 10% of each pay check to God. It is the tenth part to which God lays claim.

The difference between the tithe and the first fruit offering is, the tithe is always one tenth and the first fruit offering is always the first of the best fruit.

God commands that we bring the best of the first fruit that shows up. Numbers18:12 says, all the best of the oil, and all the best of the wine, and of the wheat, the first of them which they shall offer unto the LORD, them have I given thee. If there were defects within the first that showed up, they were to bring the best of the first unto the Lord.

Tithing and sacrificial giving are still God's ways to finance the Kingdom agenda. The Bible says:

> [10]*Bring your full tithe to the Temple treasury so there will be ample provisions in my Temple. Test me in this and see if I don't open up heaven itself to you and pour out blessings beyond your wildest dreams.*
>
> *Malachi 3:10 (MSG)*

As stewards of God's property, we must pay tithes. Jesus affirmed that tithing is a spiritual discipline that must continue to be practiced under the new covenant. The tithe is essential to the Kingdom of God and is used to support its mission of preaching the gospel throughout the whole earth as Jesus commanded. First fruit is not the method God has established to finance the church. First fruit has always had a two-fold purpose: to release praises of God for all He has done and to release more blessings from God for your obedience in trusting Him with the offering.

In every kingdom, there is a tax exacted upon the people. As citizens of the United States of America, we are all too familiar with paying taxes. Every year we file an income tax return wherein we report what we have earned and pay taxes to the federal government accordingly. Similarly, as citizens of the Kingdom of God, the tithe is your tax for living in the Kingdom and supporting its operation, maintenance, and outreach.

First Fruit Opens Doors

A knock came to my office door the other day. A sound technician was there to install equipment for a pending concert and needed to enter the front door of the sanctuary. When I opened one side, he immediately requested the other side be opened as well. His reason was that all of the equipment simply couldn't fit through the single door opening.

The difference between tithing and first fruit is, tithing only opens one door, but first fruit gets the other door opened. There are some blessings that will come forth that will require the hand of the Lord and first fruit offerings unleash those blessings.

Malachi 3:8-11 puts it this way:

> *8Will a man rob God? Yet ye have robbed me. But ye say, wherein have we robbed thee? In tithes and offerings. 9Ye are cursed with a curse: for ye have robbed me, even this whole nation. 10Bring ye all the tithes into the storehouse, that there may be meat in mine house, and prove me now herewith, saith the LORD of hosts, if I will not open you the windows of heaven, and pour you out a blessing, that there shall not be room enough to receive it. 11And I will rebuke the devourer for your sakes, and he shall not destroy the fruit of your ground; neither shall your vine cast her fruit before the time in the field, saith the LORD of hosts. 12And all nations shall call you*

> *blessed: for ye shall be a delightsome*
> *land, saith the LORD of hosts.*
> *Malachi 3:8-11 (KJV)*

Both the tithes and first fruit offerings are holy unto the Lord. There are special blessings that flow as a result of one's obedience to tithing and first fruit giving.

As citizens of the Kingdom of God, He requires us to tithe on all of our income. After sowing our first fruit seed and reaping the harvest, we must be good stewards of all that remains.

To use another illustration to distinguish between the two, I'll use my house as an example.

Like most modern homes today, my home

shares a similar design in that, although there's a perfectly accessible front door, we primarily enter the house through the garage. At one point, I had become so comfortable with entering my home through the garage, that I lost my front door key. However, there was no great rush for me to replace my lost key. After all, who needs a front door key when the garage *is* the front door?

As fate would have it, one night I entered the garage, as I always did, only to find that the door to enter the house was locked. Someone from inside the house - probably my little girl - had locked the deadbolt and I couldn't get in.

Once I got past the frustration of being locked

out of my own house, I began to look around. To my surprise, I realized that if a person *really* had to live in the garage, they could survive fairly painlessly. Just about everything they would need was in there: a freezer, a grill, a washer and dryer, reverse cycle air conditioner, clothes, bikes, cars, and more. Although one could survive in the garage, the conditions are still far from ideal. Garages serve their purpose, but they are no substitute for a house!

When it comes to giving, tithing gets you into the garage, but first fruit gets you in the house!

Understand that God is serious about our lives being in order. That's why the time is now for His people to become as knowledgable about first fruit as they are about tithing. But, it's not enough to simply know about it. The state of our world today demands that we, as Christians, fully align ourselves and our giving with the Word of God.

The act of first fruit offerings has been understudied and overlooked for far too long. At this appointed time, we must grasp the full meaning of "first things first." When you don't put first things first, everything in your life is out order. In the Gospel of Matthew, chapter 6 verse 33, Jesus said, "But seek first his kingdom and his righteousness, and all these things will be given to you as well."

The great theologian John Wesley said, "When the Possessor of heaven and earth brought you into being and placed you in this world, He placed you here not as an owner but as a steward. He entrusted you for a season with goods of various kinds, but the sole property of these still rests in Him, nor can ever be alienated from Him. As you are not your own but His, likewise it is so with all you enjoy."[1]

To further emphasize that both tithing and first fruit offerings are honorable, the following scriptures mention the two principles together:

> [37]*Moreover, we will bring to the storerooms of the house of our God, to the priests, the first of our ground meal, of our grain offerings, of the fruit of all our trees and of our new wine and olive oil. And we will bring a tithe of our crops to the Levites, for*

*it is the Levites who collect the tithes
in all the towns where we work.*

Nehemiah 10:37 (NKJV)

*[26]But the firstborn of the
animals, which should be the LORD's
firstborn, no man shall dedicate;
whether it is an ox or sheep, it is the
LORD's. [27]And if it is an unclean
animal, then he shall redeem it
according to your valuation, and
shall add one-fifth to it; or if it
is not redeemed, then it shall be
sold according to your valuation.
[28]Nevertheless no devoted offering
that a man may devote to the LORD
of all that he has, both man and beast,
or the field of his possession, shall
be sold or redeemed; every devoted
offering is most holy to the LORD.
[29]No person under the ban, who*

may become doomed to destruction among men, shall be redeemed, but shall surely be put to death. [30]And all the tithe of the land, whether of the seed of the land or of the fruit of the tree, is the LORD's. It is holy to the LORD.

Leviticus 27:26-30 (NKJV)

[5]As soon as the commandment was circulated, the children of Israel brought in abundance the firstfruit of grain and wine, oil and honey, and of all the produce of the field; and they brought in abundantly the tithe of everything.

2 Chronicles 31:5 (NKJV)

PRAYER

Father, we have been introduced to a lot of information in this book. Help us to understand the concepts of first fruit and tithing. Enable us to be good stewards of the resources you have given us. Cause us to be better stewards, to be cheerful and willing givers in a way that will please you. In Jesus name, Amen.

Chapter 7
The Promise of
First Fruit Giving

There are many promises that come with being a first fruit giver. We have made reference to the plentiful barns and bursting wine skins in Proverbs 3:10, which speak of God's abundant provision in every area of our lives. In addition, the Bible also gives us examples of how first fruit offerings activated miraculous promises.

The Story of Hannah

This first book of Samuel opens with the cry of Hannah, a godly woman. While the people cry for a king, Hannah cries for a child. Eli, the high priest, thinks Hannah is drunk as she prays before the tabernacle in Shiloh. When he discovers her true anxiety for a child, he blesses her.

Samuel was born to Hannah and, in fulfillment of her vow, she took him to Eli, the man of God.

Samuel was Hannah's first fruit unto God. He was the first to break through the womb and she offered him back to God. When Hannah took her offering to the Lord, she kept her vow to God. Her decision to give her son completely to the service of the Lord is an indisputable, immeasurable offering.

If Hannah was the mother of many children prior to this, then parting with one of many would not have been such an act of devotion. However, presenting to the Lord her one and only son, whom she loved dearly, for the service of the tabernacle, was an act of great virtue.

The miraculous occurred after Hannah resigned Samuel, her first child, to God. God subsequently blessed her with five through the effect of Eli's prayer. She bore three sons and two daughters. The Bible says, and it is true, the Lord will repay you a hundred-fold for giving unto him (Matthew 19:29).

THE STORY OF ELIJAH AND THE RAVEN

Another biblical example of God's miraculous promises fulfilled is shown in the story of Elijah and Raven. The passage of I Kings, chapter 17, opens with one of the greatest prophets to ever represent the Lord, Elijah, confronting the evil King Ahab.

In the previous chapter we learn that Ahab did more evil in the sight of God than all the kings of Israel which were before him. He not only worshipped the god Baal, but built an altar for him in the temple in Samaria (I Kings16: 30-33).

Elijah boldly walked into the palace and gave the king and queen an unfavorable "weather report." In Luke 4:25-27, Elijah told them that God was going to cut off the water for an undetermined amount of time. In the meantime, God directed Elijah to hide near the brook called Cherith.

Note that in this passage, there were two droughts, one of which is obvious - the drought caused by the absence of water. The second drought was the absence of the Word while Elijah was in hiding.

By leaving public ministry, Elijah created a second drought in the land. The absence of God's Word in our lives always creates a spiritual drought! The book of Deuteronomy puts it this way:

> *2God's Word to His people is like the rain showers from heaven.*

> *Deuteronomy 32:2*

The book of Isaiah adds that the Word is essential to our spiritual lives (Isaiah 55:10).

In spite of, God used two methods to sustain Elijah in the wilderness. One was by natural means - the brook. The other way by supernatural means - the ravens came and fed him. This is supernatural because ravens are ravenous, devouring, birds of prey. In the natural, they were more likely to have stripped Elijah's flesh off of his bones and picked his eyes out (Psalms 30:17). Ravens were considered unclean and voracious birds that were unfit for consumption. They were known to neglect their own offspring. Yet, at the will of God, they fed the prophet Elijah.

The Ravens took Elijah bread and flesh in the

morning, and bread and flesh in the evening. The prophet did not question the provisions. He gave thanks. The Lord's prayer says, "Give us this day, our daily bread." The story of Elijah and the Raven illustrates how we are to depend on God for daily provision.

PRAYER

Dear Lord Jesus, we thank you so much for all of your many blessings toward us. Your mercies are new every morning and your grace is sufficient. Please help us to focus on the promises which you have given to us in your Word. Forgive us of all our unrighteous acts and restore unto us the joy of thy salvation. And manifest in our lives, the breakthrough power of first fruit giving. In your name, we pray. Amen.

First Fruit Testimonies

When my husband began to share the revelation of first fruit, I knew it was sent to him directly from the Lord. God began to use him immediately and in mighty ways, to touch and transform the lives of believers all across the country.

It wasn't always easy for him. Yet, he persevered and allowed the Lord to use him to create new "barns filled with plenty" for those who were willing to trust God with their first fruit seed.

I was excited to sow my first fruit seed as well. I put it into the anointed hands of my priest/pastor and he waved it before God in our behalf. I am a witness with evidence that God has increased every area of our lives - financially, physically, mentally, emotionally, and spiritually.

I am a 12-year survivor of breast cancer and I'm believing God for continual good reports. Thank you pastor for allowing the Lord to use you to spread the good news of first fruit throughout the kingdom!

1st Lady D
Miami, FL

PROTECTION

When I first heard pastor Jackson teach on first fruit, I knew I had to sow a seed on behalf of my boys. Trying to raise my children among the negative elements of the streets was no small endeavor. They were good boys, but often made unwise decisions because of their associations.

I have always prayed and fasted for them, but this revelation of first fruit was another way for God to show Himself mighty in our lives.

My husband and I sowed our first revenue stream as our offering. Not many days later, we received an early morning call - the dread of every mother with children who are out of the house. Our son was being detained by police not too far from our home. As we rushed to the scene, I prayed to God about my first fruit seed.

When we arrived, our son was sitting in a squad car handcuffed. My heart skipped a beat, as I could see his troubled face. As it turned out, his cousin had been jumped by a group of boys and my son and his friends were riding around trying to find them. One of the young men fired a weapon into the air, drawing the attention of an observing officer.

All of the boys were detained and were about to be taken downtown. When my son's eyes caught mine, he burst into tears. He was trying to tell me he didn't do anything wrong. We pointed upward, motioning for him to pray to God.

At that moment, I put a demand on the seed that I had sown for my boys. "Lord, you promised if I sowed *that seed and my priest/pastor would wave it before you in my behalf, that the blessings would remain in my household!"*

As I cried out to God, an amazing thing happened. One of the officers saw me praying and said to the arresting officer, "We tested that boy's hands to be sure no powder from the fired weapon was on them. Let him go home with his mother," he said.

Wow! What an awesome God we serve! I shouted all over the streets that morning! I knew without a doubt that my first fruit seed had covered my son. One of the officers actually told me that "all four of those boys were headed downtown." You can't make me doubt Him, I know too much about Him!

Jackie
Miami, FL

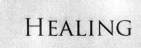

HEALING

To God be all the glory for Pastor Jackson and the teaching of The Breakthrough Power of First Fruit Giving! I have been a first fruit giver ever since Pastor Jackson shared the revelation several years ago. I am a witness with evidence of the blessings of planting first fruit seed!

Since I received the revelation and became a first fruit giver, not only have I been blessed, but my children, grandchildren, and family have been blessed as well! Truly the blessing is resting on my house according to Ezekiel 44:30.

I haven't had a secular job for 14 years and the blessings of first fruit giving has allowed me to stay debt free. Also, both of my daughters, LaKeisha and

Lonnitris, have received promotions and pay increases every year since I became a first fruit giver and neither of them are first fruit givers yet! To God be the glory!

My greatest testimony on the blessing of being a first fruit giver is concerning my son, Lonnie, Jr. In January 2008, I gave my first fruit and declared the promise of Ezekiel 44:30. On August 15, 2008, my son - who was 22 years old at that time - was admitted to the hospital for 21 days.

He was on life support and had been diagnosed with Bi-lateral Pneumonia, Congestive Heart Failure, and Respiratory Failure. He also has Sickle Cell Disease. While in the hospital, he also developed Altered Mental Status - 30 second seizure activity - which cut off the oxygen to his brain. As a result, he lost memory and also experienced altered mental status and delirium.

My son was on 14 different medications. There were 20 doctors on the case and none of them believed he would live to make it out of the hospital. They also predicted that if he did survive, he would deteriorate and die young. They said they had done all that they could do. I had to choose whose report I would believe. His medical treatment amounted to over $1 million dollars.

I reminded the Lord that I was a first fruit giver and that He promised He would cause the blessing to rest on me, my children and entire household. I stood on the promise of God. I decreed and declared that by Jesus' stripes my son was healed and he "shall live and not die," and declare the works of the Lord.

Pastor Jackson came to the hospital and prayed for my son. The Lord delivered him out of the hospital and healed him completely. He is not on any medication, he is working full time and celebrated his 27th birthday on Christmas Day 2012! To God be the glory! Those are the powerful blessings of first fruit giving and there are many more.

On January 1, 2012, I gave my first fruit, and on that same day my mother was admitted to the hospital for eight days. The doctors could not stop the bleeding nor could they find the cause. Several times during her hospital stay, she was at the point of death.

She had a total of seven blood transfusions. Again, I reminded the Lord that I was a first fruit giver and He said He would cause the blessing to rest on me and my house hold, which includes my mother and my entire family.

Like I did for my son, I declared that my mother

"shall live and not die" and declare the works of the Lord, and that by Jesus' stripes, she was healed! Once again, Pastor Jackson came to the hospital and prayed for my mother. To God be the glory! The bleeding finally stopped and my mother was released. She has not experienced any more bleeding since!

These are just a few of the testimonies I have from being a first fruit giver and the blessings continue to rest on me and my household. Truly, I am so thankful to God for giving my Pastor the revelation of The Breakthrough Power of First Fruit Giving, and anointing him to teach with authority, boldness, and clarity! To God be the glory!

Minister Debra P. Baker
Miami, FL

FINANCIAL

Prior to coming to Second Baptist, I didn't recall a sermon, to say nothing of teaching, on first fruit. That's not to say I hadn't read it in the scripture, but apparently I overlooked it. During the Fall 2009, Pastor Jackson did concentrated teaching on being blessed in the kingdom of God through first fruit giving. I had been a consistent tither for several years and knew the spiritual and material blessing from that, but first fruit was new.

Believing that God would remain faithful, I gave my first fruit offering for the first time in January 2010. It was the first payment I received on my first contract for my new business. I took deep breaths when I wrote the check, but when I released it into Pastor Jackson's hand, I knew I had taken a big-girl step of faith.

Five months later, the amount of the contract was tripled. They asked me if I would take on more responsibilities for the work and gave me a 25% increase! I thank God for Pastor Jackson and his obedience, consistency, faithfulness, and passion for the call on his life.

Betty
North Augusta, SC

Praise God everybody! When I received the teaching on first fruit giving, I was excited to take God at His Word and get my seed out of my hands and into the hands of my pastor. I'm on a fixed income and didn't know how God was going to get the harvest to me. However, my first fruit blessing came shortly afterwards in the mail from the I. R. S. - before filing my taxes!

Effie
Miami, FL

ENTREPRENEURIAL

*When I heard my pastor, Rev. Alphonso Jackson, Sr.,
teach on putting God first through first fruit giving, I
didn't have a job. However, I heard him say repeatedly,
"If it's in your heart, God will put it in your hand."*

*I promised the Lord that I would sow a first fruit
seed if He blessed me with a job. God did even more
than that! He not only gave me a job, but also allowed
me to start my own business! I gladly sowed my first
fruit seed to Pastor Jackson. He waved it to God on my
behalf. I now have a crew of men who work for me!
What a mighty God we serve!*

*Mark
Miami, FL*

I thank God for leading Pastor Alphonso Jackson to reveal "The Breakthrough Power of First Fruit Giving." The teaching has been a blessing not only to me, but to my entire household. I shared with my daughter, the teaching I received on first fruit. Her church was asking its members to give first fruit, but she was thoroughly confused on what that meant.

I purchased some of Pastor Jackson's sermons on CD and we devoted several hours in study and research throughout the week. Tithing was something she has done for years, but this past January, through faith, she gave her first fruit offering. The business she started a few years ago has began to flourish through networking opportunities and increased exposure. We are grateful for the breakthrough power of first fruit giving!

Quilan
Miami, FL

FAMILY

In January 2007, after hearing Pastor Jackson teach his congregation about first fruit, I wrestled with God before finally deciding to be obedient. I gave my entire first check of the year to my Bishop, the late Bishop Larry D. Manning, Sr. At the time, I was believing God for a son. I didn't get pregnant that year, but God blessed me with double the amount of the first fruit that I had given my Bishop.

A year later, in January of 2008, I didn't have to wrestle with God because I saw what God could or would do based on the previous year. I, again, gave my Bishop my first check of the year believing God for a son. Bishop Manning waved my first fruit offering before the Lord and came into agreement with me that God would give us a son that year.

In September of that year, we found out that we were pregnant! God did what the doctors said couldn't nor wouldn't be done, but that's not all. A month after finding out we were pregnant, we found out that we were having twins!

God gave us double for the trouble and the blessings didn't stop. A couple of months later, in December 2008, we found out that not only were we having one son, but God had blessed us with two!

God bless you Pastor Jackson. You have been an integral part in my boys' manifestation. If it had not been for your teaching, I would not ever have stepped out on faith and given that entire check. You are truly an anointed man of God who teaches about first fruit as I have never heard it taught before!

Trice
Valdosta, GA

ABUNDANCE

The principle of First Fruit is a truth that has completely revolutionized my life. Since childhood, I have been taught about the importance of giving. However, it wasn't until I heard the revelation of first fruit giving that I had some serious questions and concerns.

As a young man who was just starting to mature in Christ, it didn't make much sense to give away my entire check. Nevertheless, that's when I realized that I had to change my mindset. First fruit giving isn't about giving away money. Rather, it's about giving towards the promises that God has tailor-made just for me.

By faith, I sowed my first fruit seed to God, and it seemed as if God literally opened up a celestial window of heaven and rained down every kind of blessing into my life. Since that initial gift, I've become a continual first fruiter, and I've seen God move in a mighty way in every area of my life. I am a strong believer in the breakthrough power of First Fruit giving, not just because it's a principle that I was taught by my pastor, but because God has shown Himself faithful to me as a result of my faithfulness to Him.

I challenge you to try this principle and watch God transform your life, as He has mine. You won't be disappointed!

Rev. Al Jackson, Jr.
Princeton, FL

Each year, whenever my pay increased or when a new year began, I would faithfully give my first fruit offering. After resigning from a 20-year career, based on a technicality, I was denied compensation that I was previously told I would receive. I fought to receive this money for a couple of years. Then my Pastor told me to forgive and let go of my pursuit! He said "God will repay."

Years later, I began a new job and received my first commissions check on December 22nd, just a few days before Christmas. I sowed my first fruit offering. Two weeks later, I received my second commissions check, which happened to also be my first check of the New Year. It, too, became a first fruit offering! This time,

I wrestled with giving two checks in a row, but I resolved that I never had been able to beat God's giving nor His goodness. So again, I offered my first fruit onto the Lord.

That same year, God set it up and allowed my former boss - who was then a candidate for a position in the city - to stop by our Sunday worship service to campaign. It was then that I realized that I was still bitter and angry and had not forgiven him. But, it was a divine set up.

God gave me the opportunity to finally forgive and let go of what happened. After service, I finally walked over to him, greeted him and forgave him. At that moment, the peace of God that surpasses all understanding began to flood my soul. I could never express adequately how God saved my very life on that day during that very moment.

About two weeks later, my daughter walked in with the mail and said, "Mommy, it is a letter for you from Miami Dade County." I opened the letter and inside was a check dated seven years earlier! This check was my initial compensation check, but it, also included seven years of interest, which totaled $54,389.12. God gave me double for my troubles! Double the first fruit – double the blessing!

There are many more first fruit offering blessings I can boast in the Lord about, but this by far appeared to be the most sacrificial, and certainly one of the most rewarding spiritually, emotionally and financially! To God be the glory!

Minister Rhonda F. Lewis
Miami,
FL

A few years ago I was working in the mortgage and real estate industry. However, after the market crashed, I was forced to close my business and sell my home. I literally had no income. While attending Second Baptist Church, under the leadership of Rev. Dr. Alphonso Jackson, Sr., I began to see giving in a whole different light.

I had been a faithful tither since 1978, but in 2008, I heard Pastor Jackson teach on first fruit giving. It was a difficult time in my life as I had not only closed my business and sold my home, but I was also facing a divorce and making decisions that were trying my faith.

I told God I would take Him at His Word and would walk by faith and not by sight. In January 2009,

I received a small check in the mail. It was all that I had received in months, yet I sowed it as my first fruit offering. I was so excited to be able to walk up to Pastor Jackson on that Sunday morning and give my gift.

Out of obedience to the man of God and my love for Jesus, I was offered a job on April 1, 2009. Not only was I offered a job in the church that I fell in love with, but God also opened up other doors for me.

I was able to get another car, as my previous car had been repossessed. However, most importantly, doors in ministry began to open. Through first fruit giving, God taught me that when I am faithful to Him with the little, He will be the provider of much. I also saw from this experience that I could never out-give God. The more I give to Him, the more He gives back to me. To God to the glory!

Rose
Highpoint , NC

When I first heard the principle of first fruit giving, I was so encouraged that I couldn't wait until my next increase so that I would have an opportunity to activate God's promise. Several months later, I received the first bonus check of my career. I gave it to my Pastor and walked away in faith.

That same year, I received a promotion and a large pay increase. When I received my first paycheck after the promotion, I separated the amount that reflected the increase and gave it to my Pastor again as a first fruit offering. The second bonus check of my career was three times as much as the one I gave as a first fruit!

God is never slack concerning His promises. I

believe that a portion of God's consistent favor in my life can be attributed to first fruit seed that He has allowed me to plant over the years.

Rev. Robert J. Brooks, Jr., Senior Pastor
St. Peters Missionary Baptist Church
Miami, FL

I am indeed blessed to be under the leadership of Pastor Alphonso Jackson, Sr. Through his teaching the Word of God, I can say that I have grown by leaps and bounds for the Kingdom of God. I have been under Pastor Jackson's leadership for the past eight years and he began teaching the first fruit principle shortly after I joined Second Baptist Church.

At a time when pastors were rarely teaching about tithes and offering, Pastor Jackson went a step further and introduced the first fruit principle to the congregation. Pastor Jackson encouraged the congregation to take God at His Word. This would indeed be a faith walk for the people of God.

I, along with many others, decided to take God

at His Word through the vessel of Pastor Jackson. I was set to receive a raise in the following month after learning about first fruit. I decided to trust God and give the increase as a first fruit offering unto God.

As time went on that year, I forgot about the seed that I had sown at the beginning of the year, however, the Lord remembered. He caught up with His Word. By November, I received a promotion into an administrative position. It is important to understand that I did not interview for this position. The Lord showed me favor and I knew it was directly due to my seed!

I began to give God the first fruit of my lips through prayer, early each morning. Due to this time of consecration, the Lord began to line up my days according to His Word. I began to apply the first fruit principle to every aspect of my life.

Today, this principle still applies to my life. My children, ages nine and four, apply this principle to their lives. They don't know anything different. One can say that they were born and raised following the Word of the Lord. He is indeed pouring out His blessings that I don't have room enough to receive!

What the Lord is doing for the body of Christ through the man of God, Pastor Alphonso Jackson, Sr., is marvelous in my eyes!

Ericka
Miami, FL

NOTES

Chapter 6

1. Illustrations Unlimited, a Topical Collection of
Hundreds of Stories, Quotatios, & Humor
for Speakers, Writers, Pastors, and Teachers.
James Hewitt,   Editor.Tyndale House
Publishers: Later Printing edition (July 15,
1988).

REVEREND DR.
ALPHONSO JACKSON, SR.

Rev. Alphonso Jackson, Sr. is the Senior Pastor/Teacher of Second Baptist Church, the "Church in the Heart of the Community, with the Community at Heart."

Rev. Jackson preached his initial sermon in August of 1980 at New Shiloh Baptist Church, under the leadership of his father, Reverend Dr. Arthur Jackson, Jr. In that same year, he began a 20-year teaching career with Miami Dade County Public Schools. In 1993, he was honored as the *Teacher of the Year.*

As Youth Pastor of New Shiloh, from 1981

to 1984, Pastor Jackson's uncompromising and bold teaching of God's Word changed the lives of many people. The Lord continued to find favor in him. In 1985, he became the Senior Pastor of St. James Baptist Church in Coconut Grove, FL. He served St. James faithfully for over 16 years.

Noted as a community leader, Rev. Jackson currently serves as Moderator of the Seaboard Baptist Missionary Association of Florida, Inc., as well as Second Vice President of the Florida General Baptist Convention, Inc. He is also the Director of Finance for the Florida General Baptist Convention. Additionally, Rev. Jackson is also Chairman of the Children's Learning Center Board of Directors and is a member of the National Association for the Advancement of Colored People (NAACP) and People United to Lead the Struggle for Equality (PULSE). He is also the President of Richmond Heights Community Alliance.

Rev. Jackson has served on the Board of Directors for Coconut Grove Cares and One Church One Child. Additionally, he is the former President of the Elizabeth Verrick Restoration Committee.

In 2004, Pastor Jackson was awarded an Honorary Doctor of Divinity from Saint Thomas Christian College. He earned his Bachelor of Arts Degree in Elementary Education in 1980 at Olivet Nazarene University (Kankakee, IL). Rev. Jackson completed graduate studies at Florida Memorial

College, (Miami, FL) and advanced seminary studies at the Interdenominational Theological Center (Atlanta, GA).

In 1984, Rev. Jackson married the love of his life, the former Dewana Williams. He is the proud father of two children, Alphonso, Jr. and Brianna.

CPSIA information can be obtained at www.ICGtesting.com
Printed in the USA
LVOW12s1216250813

349510LV00001B/1/P